Lessons

Lessons

Charles M. Jasak

RESOURCE *Publications* · Eugene, Oregon

LESSONS

Resource Publications
An Imprint of Wipf and Stock Publishers
199 W. 8th Ave., Suite 3
Eugene, OR 97401

www.wipfandstock.com

PAPERBACK ISBN: 978-1-6667-5176-5
HARDCOVER ISBN: 978-1-6667-5177-2
EBOOK ISBN: 978-1-6667-5178-9

09/08/22

This collection is dedicated to those who have learned many lessons (the hard way or the easy way) and a burning desire to learn more.

Contents

1970 Pontiac LeMans

The garage was unstable
Smells of oil, old wood and ancient dust
Filled the air
Its future was always in question
Like all futures tend to be

But that 1970 LeMans
Despite the splotches of matted gray primer
Waiting for crisp, new paint
That aggressive Thrush Muffler decal on the dashboard speedometer
Symbolic
Of the horsepower waiting to be unchained
The black interior
Disintegrating
Slowly Shedding memories
Discarding the past

The cinematic illumination
Of a father driving his 5-year-old son
Engine roaring
The windows down

When the accelerator hit the floor
Both were unwilling to acknowledge
The difference between the
Responsibility of being a man
And the reckless excitement of being a boy

But it never happened
Like that

Instead
The father's belongings
Were thrown
On the front yard
Packed in
Garbage Bags

Left was
The LeMans
And the boy

Adrift
Like the particles of dust that once
Floated through the garage
The future was empty
As if it never existed in the first place

Sometimes dreams dissipate
Remain unfinished
And

Fade

Like a 1970
Pontiac LeMans

Violence

My father was only a few feet away
I knew there was no way
I'd ever
Get away with it

That moment leading up to
The smashing of
My Foot
Through the window
Was without calculation
Without critical thought
And
Without a plan

Impulse captured me
As I walked over
To the neighbor's basement window
And destroyed it

Knowing
There was no way

Out

Shattered glass made such a sharp sound
More detestable than I hoped
Louder than I thought possible

The deliberate act
Of destruction

Pure satisfaction

As the glass trickled down to
The neighbor's basement floor

I knew that I was in trouble
But I didn't care

That's why I did it

For the first time in my life, I felt it

Without logic
Without remorse
I experienced that forbidden fruit
The euphoric sensation of

Emotionless

Authentic

Violence

Walking

Walking together
Those were my favorite times

Marching our way down
To the baseball field
As I dreamt of becoming
The next professional player

Fielding every grounder
Hitting every pitch
Signing autographs
Under
The shimmering lights
Of some big-league ballpark

These endless thoughts
Expanded in my mind
Boundless
Unbridled
Scattering
Like smoke

As the wind whistled
Through the plastic batting helmet
With the caricature of an Oriole
A worn image
Faded by countless hitting sessions

My glove
Always secured
Around the barrel
Of my bat
Bouncing without rhythm
Over my right shoulder
As I tactfully
Evaded
Every crack
In the sidewalk

Anticipation personified
Investing in the future

Isn't the goal always
The Hall of Fame?

But the most important
Part of this experience
Was not in the pursuit of greatness

The storied moments
Were always
Rooted
In precious time

With
My baseball gear
Avoiding cracks in the sidewalk

Walking
With my Dad

Apple

Is that what you really want?

To see
Your idols
When the world isn't watching?

The universe
Created
Destroyed?

Your god
Creator
Illusion
Executioner
. . . Lie?

How others see you
How they
Think about you
In your absence?

Your parents' dreams
Their Mistakes
Their Secrets?

Civilizations
Born
Demolished
And Forgotten?

Your enemies
Your friends
Unable to tell the difference?

One man's success
Is
Another's failure

And
Those without a chance
To experience either

Do you want to
Know it all?

Ecstasy
Pain
Euphoria

Enchantment?

Then take a bite

Savor its unpleasantness

. . . And know

Unrequited

It was the lunch room
Where I first saw her

Wearing a black shirt
With a screen-printed
Dragon

Sparkles
and
Silver ink

She didn't walk
She floated
Like a ghost
Untouchable

Producing fear
Pins
Like thousands of ants
Like chaos
Like premonition

Beautiful
Like Oleander
Consuming
Like the Black Widow
Luring
Like a Siren

And I followed
The seductive aroma
The intoxicating sounds
The venomous beauty

To share a dance
A kiss
A memory
A moment

Only to watch it
Splinter
Into a million
Stinging fragments

But
I
Can never
Be
Broken

Again

Work

Can you come in this weekend?
Spare a few hours away from your family?

. . . To make me rich?

Run
Lift
Sweat
Build
Break

For your

Payment
. . . Scraps
Split amongst the heard

I appreciate your time
Your effort

For

My homes
My cars
My vacations
My savings
My boat

My ability

. . . To not have to . . .

As I sip on my margarita
Tranquil
Knowing that the work will get done
By you

Knowing that you are content
Receiving the leftovers
Unwanted
From my profits

From my luxury

From my comfort

You are . . .
As so many are willing
. . . To work

Appreciative
I relax
Knowing
That you are . . .

My infinitely
Replaceable

Inferior

Live

Check your feed
Check your views
Check your likes
Check your vanity

Your weakness is sickening
Your desire to be loved
But never judged

You'll post anything
You'll say anything
You'll become whatever they want
To avoid their glaring recognition
... The disintegration of your "soul"

But

If you post the picture
The message
The everlasting wisdom
The pliable, plastic smile

Think like they do
Look as they say
Do what they demand
Work where you should
How they would
... maybe they'll like you

Or they won't

It makes no difference

As long as they
Hit the "like" button

Mom

She sat there
Weeping

Was she regretting her decisions?
Reflecting on her actions?

Doubtful

Considering homicide
Suicide
Cheating
One more sip
Perhaps?

Undoubtedly
She must be
Thinking about
How
Everyone blames her
For her self-inflicted wounds
Her instability
Her self-medication

Maybe
She was frustrated
At the way her hands felt

After ravaging
Beating
Throwing
Ripping the hair
Of a child

Maybe her vocal cords burned
After the shouting

Scorched from the volume
The incendiary resentment
Of ever
. . . Giving birth in the first place

But

Everything he's ever done
Has been with the intent
Of being the exact opposite
Of you

Everything that you are

A

Manipulative
Lonely
Pathetic

Damaged frame
With no picture
And no purpose

Betrayal

I'll never forget that crazy character

Figment

Or the ride
At
Disneyland
. . . The magic

A silly purple dragon
Full of colors
Full of joy
Full of fondness

But when
We got home

I hated the stuffed toy

I told you
That I wanted to live with my dad
In our 3 room
Second floor
Deteriorated
Apartment
Where you proceeded to try
To push me out through the particle board door

"Then go," you spoke

As you grabbed me by my hair
Pulling
Dragging
Failing to have the strength
To shove me out
Down the stairs

So you threw it
The make-believe Figment
The imagination
The memory
To the bottom of the steps

You said..

It's ok
I'm all done
You can go get it

You let me go
You
Calmed your voice

And at 6 years old . . .
I believed you

I willingly walked out
Down each stair

Arrived at the bottom
At
The Figment
The extinguished joy
Rotted Reminiscence

And
I picked it up

Looked up at you

As you shut the door
Behind me
. . . And locked it

Memory

It was the first time
I had cried
In my adult life

I made sure
That
I had made it
To my car
Before the first tear

I waited
Until the funeral was over
When
Where
No one could see me

It's hard to pinpoint what it was . . .

Maybe it was the time
We all bought fake mustaches
And
Walked around the city

Or when you ate the plant
At Denny's
At 2 a.m.

When you gave a beautiful girl
At the ice cream shop
A dime
And casually thanked her for the night before
(When we all knew you had no chance)

Maybe it was the punk shows
Hundreds of them
Where
We lost our voices
Our hearing
And our ignorance

Or the time you rubbed
Muscle cream on your giggle berries
And thought a hot shower would make it better
(Bad idea)

Perhaps it was the funeral
Seeing the people
I hadn't seen forever
Who
All shared
The best
And worst
Of times

But more than likely

It was the fact that your band played
Your brother sang
For the first time
. . . Last time
Without you

Or maybe it was
When those closest to you
Let out
Screams of affliction
Clutched the ashes
Refusing to let go

Like there was a way they could change it

Or
How the rose petals
Floated down the river
Beside your ashes
Flowing
Sinking
Disappearing

I guess I was
Just thinking
How things used to be
And how life
Was better
When you were
In it

Self-Incarceration

Right
... the doctor said
They happen
For no good reason

The room simply starts spinning
Snapping the deep sleep

With pressure in your head
Salty pools in your palms
Sirens in your ears

And you can't breathe
Even if you tried
A heart attack?
At least that would explain the
Scorching chest pain
Or the inferno
In your rib cage

The rapid
Irregular
Unpredictable
Heartbeat

But it doesn't explain
The desire to jump out of bed
When perfectly safe
Secure
Unrecognizable in the mind
And you contemplate hurdling
Sprinting
To
Anywhere
To
No where

Terrified
Of what underlying disease
Is causing such sensations
Such sweat

Do I have a heart condition?
A growth on my brain that
Causes irrational reactions?
A hormonal imbalance?
Maybe some sort of blood disorder?
A clot?
PTSD?

Surely it's something explainable
Something
That could be diagnosed
By experts

I mean, what else
Would feel this way?

The final moments?
The last breath?
The final weak

Hasty
Ruptured
Pulsation

It lasts for seconds
Fewer
Than you can
Fathom

One
Click of the clock
That moves leisurely
Like eternity

Moving forever
Moving like Panic

Roots

A tree is fixed
Its roots deeply driven
Intertwined
Never moving

Yet it grows
Taller
Wider
The leaves capturing sunlight
Rain
When the sky decides to give such gifts

Powerless
It sways
Helpless
As the wind blows
Sometimes gently
Sometimes violently
Sometimes tyrannically

Yet it grows
From the top
Its branches stretching
Limbs reaching
As far as they can
But never far enough to see more
Learn more

Experience more
As the roots
Anchor the
Stationary
Prisoner
Prevent the tree from
Ever moving
From leaving safety

Yet it grows
Reaching
But failing to
Touch
Anything

As it settles
Planted
Secure
Ignorant
Enslaved

But . . .
Just imagine
How much a tree
Could grow
If it were free

Freedom

Like the wind blowing
Through the car window
On a sunny day
When the temperature is just right
Enjoy it

Bask in . . .
Hating religion
Those damned people
And their
God
Or even worse
Those with no God at all

Find pleasure in
Despising cigarettes
Or smoking three packs a day
Black-lungged

Find solace
In
Loathing guns
The right for citizens to defend themselves
Against tyranny
Against people like you
Or
Ever so simply
Choose not to buy one

Feel repulsed by abortions
Never having been forced
To make such a choice
Or
Politely
Choose not to have one

Feel uncomfortable with homosexuality
Or fly the rainbow colors
Celebrate the marriage
Between Adam and Eve
While also choosing
To celebrate
Or not celebrate
The marriage
Of Adam and Steve

Feel the freedom of . . .

A Christmas tree
A Menorah
A basket of fruit
An upside down crucifix
Or Pentagram tattooed on your
Forearm
Forehead
Your left ass cheek

Right next to the American Bald Eagle
And the universal sign of masculinity

After going to church
Or worshipping Satan
During the Christmas season
Or Hanukkah season

Or whatever season
Your cult
Chooses for this time of year

As you leave the church
Synagogue
Mosque
Temple
Satanic Monastery
Parking lot

Routinely
Drive
To the bar
A gay bar
With your heterosexual partner
Who may be
Your
Homosexual partner
Or unidentified person who isn't your partner at all
And drink an appletini
Observe people of all colors
Genders
And
Some people
With
No identification
Classification
At all
Because
After all . . .
People
Are just people . . .

Listen to the music
Or don't

Talk
Argue
Agree
Fight
About politics
Religion
Race
Gender
And all of the other controversy
You should never discuss
Or
Always discuss
While carrying
Your legal
Constitutional Right
In your holster
Stamped with the
Symbol of racial equality
Gender equality
Rainbows

Sip your drink
Handed to you
By the man behind the bar
Or is it a woman?
Does it even matter?
As you
Converse
Exchange pleasantries
And
Leave a cash tip
Even in
A cashless society

But the best thing you could do
Better than anything else

Is

To

Stop what you're doing . . .

Leave people

Alone

Sit . . .

Enjoy . . .

And let others

Do the same

Skull and Crossbones

Everything that I choose to do
Is completely self-serving
The only difference between you and I
Is that I tell the truth
And
I admit it

Hiding behind
The guise of
Philanthropy
Altruism
Is truly for the weak

Instead . . .

Intimidate
Steal
Dominate
Take
For thy pocket
For thy reputation
For sheer entertainment

Disavow
The rules
The people
The deities

The social construct
All of whom
Have abandoned you

Who have stolen from you
Robbed your identity
Abused your trust
With malice
With intent
And
Watched you drown

Rather . . . .

Commandeer

Better yet . . .

Relish in

Control
Brutality
Copulation
and
Bounty

With impunity
Do as the others do
Without illusion
Without deception

Embrace the bitterness
Of victory
No lies

Hoist the Black Flag
Don't turn away
Look them all in the eye

As you

Dictate
Monopolize and
Mutilate

Stabbing them in the front . . . unapologetically

All of those

Who can only sit
Helpless
Hopeless

And watch
You take

All they've tried to withhold
From you

Regret

I was young
But I still remember
I had failed

I got onto the bus
Yellow
The color of a dandelion
The color of a coward

I walked up
The steps
To the back of the bus
Where you feel the bumps a little more
Where the cool kids sat

And they walked on the bus too
... the cool kids
Smelling of cigarettes

All the way to the back
Next to me
Behind her

She was new to the school
She had been there for a month
Maybe two
And no one knew the sound of her voice
I never even learned her name

Even on that day
She was silent
As she sat
Still
Clearly shy
Clearly in poverty
As she often wore
The same clothes
Never a brand name anyone would recognize

That day
It was green sweatpants
With tight elastics
That squeezed high against her shin

And a black jacket
Warm
Safe from the New England cold

And as she sat
The girl behind her
Grabbed a pair of scissors
From her bag

The older boys
Much older than me
Much bigger
Much stronger
Began to snicker

The girl reached out her hand
Bringing the blades
Closer to the girl's jacket
Without fear
Consequence
Or remorse

And she began to cut holes
Indiscriminately
Jumping from one part of the black coat
Slice
To the next
Slice
And the next

Laughter grew amongst the group
Louder
More maniacal
With each act of vandalism
Each sound of laceration
Against the
Snug
Fragile
Fibers

Enraged
I could feel my face burn with indignation
My stomach churned with disgust
My fists started to contract into
Round
Sweating
Weapons
As my mind composed visions
Of
Unrelenting
Justified
Vigilantism

And they laughed

Like I wasn't even there
Like no one
Was there

Like no one
Would do anything
To stop them
From cackling
From making another cut
Exposing the white fluff
Exposing the intrinsic torment
The whimpering
Of the girl

And still I sat
Motionless
Afraid
Knowing that if I stood
If I spoke
Larger
Intimidating boys
Smelling like tobacco
Would stand
Change their target
And push me
Punch me

So I chose neutrality
And
Embarrassingly
Did nothing

But it was the last time

I stood idle

And watched the oppressor win

Shell

That's usually all that remains
After weakness enters

Once it's inside
The disease spreads

It devours
Disintegrates
Evaporates
Leaving the skeleton
Brittle
and Delicate

Like them

They were
Once ravenous conquerors
Focused on expansion
Focused on strength
Focused on war

And then . . .
Came success
Followed by
Apathy

They were no longer hungry
Which ensured
They'd eventually be
Left starving and
Emaciated

All that was possible was achieved
Everything they ever wanted
Peace
Safety
Wealth
and Luxury

Forgotten were the days of vehemence
Savagery
And desire

Rapture was replaced with
Comfort and Complacency

Power and Sacrifice
Replaced with Leisure and Convenience

Sweat and blood
Replaced with the most expensive
Food and Drink

And worse . . .

Ignorance

The final fulfillment of prosperity
Replaced the ambitious appetite

And like all things that accomplish prosperity
Like all things that find the
wished upon sanctuary
Of asylum

They became decrepit

People
Buildings
Ideas
And
Countries
Succumb to
Frailty

But the thing
About weak things
Is that they always

Break

Apex

The wolf
Eats
Without an apology

There's nothing to blame
There's no excuse

He isn't rabid
Or crazed
Or broken

With consciousness
And
Absence of conscience
He is entirely intact
Entirely aware
Of the anguish
He conceives
And does so
Enthusiastically

The beast
Is entirely mindful
Completely Familiar
With what he has done
And the excitement
To do it all again

The residual
Dripping from the mouth
Isn't saliva

It is
Blood
Clotted
Decorated with fragments of flesh
Flowing from the
Semi-satiated
Tastebuds
Of the predator

And that taste
Reminds him
Of his next meal
Before this one
Has even begun
To digest

Guiltless and Empowered
Dreaming of the next encounter
The next painful cry
The climax of impassive fangs
Shredding into veins
The sensation of
Departure
Termination
Then Silence

This euphoria
is
Quickly followed by
Indifference

The wolf does this patiently
Every day
Distant
And free

Fearing nothing
Feeling nothing
Knowing
His position
His capability
At any time
In any place
Without limitation
Without consequence
To
Repeatedly
Force his will
And eat

Cardinal

I don't believe
In any of it

It is said
When you see a cardinal
(Supposedly)
You are seeing
A deceased loved one
Coming to visit

It's all fake though

Ghosts
The Afterlife
Heaven
Hell
. . . Cardinals

Believe the lies if you want to
Who am I to say otherwise?

I was chosen
Selected
To help carry
The casket

Like each cemented step
Up to the entrance of the church
The situation was frigid
Fixed
And
Lifeless

But
That wasn't the worst part

Touch
Time
Incinerated

As we lifted the casket
I gripped the handle tight

A Death Grip

I could have if I wanted to
I could have ripped the casket out of their hands
Refused to let them push the box into the back of the car

But I didn't
I let the casket slide
The back door shut
The car drive away

But it'll be ok

I remember
The Comfort
The Support
The Love

I remember all of it . . .
When I look out the window
Watch a cardinal land on a branch
And say

It's so nice to see you again

Mountain

I had driven by it growing up
But I had never been to the top

The history of the mountain is vibrant
Guests of the Prospect House
Would travel from the Smiths Ferry Railroad Station
Full of contentment and delight
Eyes peering out of the train window
Enchanted by the beautiful
New England wilderness

Once they arrived at the base of the mountain
They'd travel up the side
In a tram

It wasn't a tram
That we drove in this time
We were in a blue Hyundai
. . . Smurf blue with
A dent in the side
An abundance of questions
Whether or not we'd make it to the top

The hotel that sits at the peak was empty
No longer in use
No longer surrounded by the people
On holiday

But that day
Its breath had returned

The orange, yellow and red
Engulfed the landscape
A Conflagration
Of Beauty
Of Mystery

We could see everything

We could see the tops of churches
Communities from afar
Too far to notice a single blemish

Flawless

Not some abstract piece of art
No intent to hide imperfections

In fact
It was perfection
Every detail
Clear
and Genuine

Places you'd seen countless times
Looked different from far away

We could see everything

Through the quaintness of towns
The humbling natural beauty of changing seasons
We could see it all

I swear we saw our first Christmas together
And the first time we would fall in love with each other's families

Right over there . . .
That's where we saw the faded yellow t-shirt
A smiley face
And a knee on the kitchen floor

On the other side of the mountain
Right over here
Was the gazebo
Filled with white
And elegant shades of pink and green
Family and friends

The ones who matter the most

We could see

The back side of the mountain
The time
I was in the bathroom
As the nurses scurried about the waiting room
Looking
Panicking
That the father would
Miss it
The introduction
The joy of our lives

But as we approached the final side
The fog began to roll in
Over the foliage
Over the peaceful communities
Obscuring the view

For I remember looking closely
Through that fog
Translucent
Saturated in autumn
Soaked in uncertainty

There was a glint

And upon a second glance
Despite the difficulty to view it all
Not knowing what would happen next
I could see

You

With
My hand
Holding yours

Caged

He looked pristine
The fur coat was
Elegant
The mane and the tail
Looked like Hollywood

Strutting
Gracefully
Around the lawn
Fabricated trees and tall grass
Carefully planted
To look like Africa
To sound Like Africa
To feel like Africa

This lion
Has no challengers
He is the king
Of the chain linked kingdom
For which he rules
He wanders without a cause

Where crowds
Can
Eagerly watch
For a fee

There are no risks
Of weather
No threat
Of adversaries

With
Endless access to water
Only bountiful
Amounts of food are available
Food that will never run
Food that will never fight back

This comfortable
Pleasurable
Life
Of longevity
And
Without worry
Belonged to those
Who fed him
Kept him preserved
Kept him safe

Only sounds of
"Mommy,
I want to see
The lion"
Disrupted the general
Silence and security

And his days
Are far safer
Than those
Of his counterpart

The Lion
Who roams the scorching grasslands
Limps
From battles won
Battles lost
Prowling
Hunting
The desiccant earth
Thirsty
For the next sip of water
Next drop of blood
Eager
To fight
To kill

Distinguished marks
Of wars
Proof
Of carnage
Every onslaught
Engraved
In the jagged lines
Of his
Ragged
Monstrous
Face

This Lion's life is
Succinct
No one to feed him
No one to insulate him

But
However brief
However laborious
He still hunts

He mates
Feeds
Rules

Boundlessly
Never having to ask anyone
For
Permission

The Mob

It always leads to destruction

Your silence
Your obedience
Is the conduit
So . . .

Willfully
Imprison yourself
Again
Build your own obstruction
And
Place your values
On the shelf

Sheepishly
Howl with the wolves
And
Submit

It's simply easier to agree
Than to believe what you see
And say what you mean

After all
Being the voice
Of opposition

Of logic
Is the despised path
Of most resistance

Uncomplicated
Is the decision
To jump
When told to jump
Sing when told
To sing

The Devil moves in a crowd
But better to follow
Than to speak too loud

As expected
You will
Fail to act
Neglect to scream the truth
Avoid
Being judged
Ridiculed
For thinking

For defying the mob

Lies

Everywhere you look
And they're always intentional

Hollow

That's how you came into this world
Leave in the same fashion

From the moment you become aware
Give of yourself
To Everyone
Everything
Around you

Leave this world
Exhausted
Feeling desolate
Dried up
From giving Time
Honesty
And Wisdom

Let your experiences
Let your actions
Leave their mark
Every second
Every day

Exhausted
When you
Feel like
You can't move another inch

Someone else will need you
To listen
To advise
To love

Don't fall for the
Illusion of fatigue
Stand
One more time
Help
One more person

Do it
Until your final moment

Expire
Hollow
With no more left to give

A candle

That is never lit
Will never burn out
And will last forever
To
Collect dust
Fade
Become dull
And forgotten

Literature

Is supposed to be
Dangerous

. . . Change my mind

I'll be the first to admit
That there are some holes
In the movie

But
The Goonies
Is a timeless
Masterpiece

The "Truffle Shuffle"
Is still better than
The YMCA
Macarena
Chicken Dance
And Electric Slide
Combined

Perfect Inaction

Is a path
To perfect failure

Imagine

Living life
Weekend
To weekend
. . . imagine

Humanity

Ever revolving
. . . Never evolving

Remember when

Society
Appreciated
Civil discourse
And difference of opinion?
. . . me either

Once

You've broken
It . . .

It is lost

And you
Will never
Get it

Back

Sons of Liberty

July 4th
Is a shadow
of April 18th

This date
Marks a moment
Of
Meaningful Action
A true test
Of
Resolve

When men
Could no longer
Sit
Idly
. . . Fearfully

There was no room
Left
For conversation
No opportunity
For peaceful
Opposition
To find common ground
To reconcile

That night . . .
The faction
Of injustice
And tyranny
Furiously
Burned
In the fires
Of freedom

Ideas
Passions
Pleas
Threats
Became
Tangible entities

All became
Reflections
In the blood
Of Rebellion

In the blood
Of promises
Kept

The first shot
Ripped through
The souls
Of each man
Woman
Child

Forcing each
To consider
Liberty
Submission

Or
Death
As the blast echoed
And encroached
The deepest recesses
Of
Every
Single
Spirit

Time had expired
Decisions had to
Be made
Without any
Assertion
Or affirmation

One had to look inside
Make the agreement
Accept responsibility
The potential
Of termination
With no assurance
Of
Independence

This was the occasion
The brief
Tic in
Time
When the
The individual
Had naivete
Torn from
The protection of
Disinterest
And ignorance

The decree
Where the exploited
Chose
Sovereignty over
Subjugation

When the Revolution
Had already
Been won

Everything was

Fine
And then
One day
I woke up
And the world
Lost its mind

This is

Chemical burn
It will hurt
More
Than you've
Ever been burned
And
You will have
A scar

The sizzling
Of searing flesh
A reminder
Of the hopelessness
Of the reality
The inevitability
Of death

But it's the scar
That
Unceasingly reminds
Of sour truths

None of them care
About you
You know

They all
Lie

The politicians
Religious leaders
Media outlets
Teachers

They told you
If you just do what they say
You will be safe
You will find salvation
You will be presented
With
Authenticity

But you won't

Consumerism
Feeds on
Your desperate
Need
For validation
And you will
Be just a character
In another
Fable

If you buy that
Perfume
You won't be
Prettier

That's the
Truth

You'll never be
That person
Whose name is on the

Bottle
Whose face is on the
Cover
No matter
How hard
You try

The government
Will never
Save you

The media
Will never
Show you

No religion
Can prove
It to you

No teacher
Can ever
Explain
Why

Once the pain stops
Once you pour
Vinegar
To neutralize
The burn
The disfigurement
On the back of your
Hand
Will remain

A memento
To remind you
That this

Is all a lie
That you
Are all
You have

Now would be the time to
Thank me
For giving you
The first
And only
Glimmer of
Honesty
Branded
In the shape
Of a
Kiss

Do you

Really
Want to live
Forever?

Parasite

Humanity
Takes
Everything
From the earth
Multiplying
Giving nothing
In return

Does it

Really matter
Anyway?

There is

Something
About pain
That connects
Us all
To each
Other

Winston

Wrote
"Down with
Big Brother"

But when
It mattered most
He squealed
Cried
Pleaded
And
Begged

You will
Too

It started

Slowly
With a faint
Whisper
Of poverty
Desperation
And Fear

The thought
Process was . . .

If I comply
This time
Things will get
Better

Things
Eventually
Get better

Right?

Each quiet
Methodical
Passing of
The clock
Failed
To recognize

Failed
To inspire
Action

Instead . . .

Hate
Blame
Division
Spite

Gestapo

Book burnings
Blind allegiance
Weapons confiscation

Indoctrination
In education

Disappearance of
Neighbors

Silence

Idleness

Deprivation
Carbon Monoxide
Inhalation
Incineration

Death

Came one
After another

And it all
Started
Slowly
With
A whisper

When she

Was born
It was
Really
The first
Time
I understood
What it meant
To place
Another
Before
Myself

What if

Your horoscope
Meant nothing

You could smash
A mirror
(Intentionally if you wanted to)

Drive peacefully
In your
Car
Until
Interrupted
By the
Crossing
Of a
Black cat

You could open
An umbrella
Indoors

Spill salt

Pick up
A penny
Tails up (gasp)

Walk under
A ladder

And have
None of
It matter

Because
All consequences
And rewards
Are a product
Of your own
Actions

And
Nothing more

He sat

There
. . . Waiting
For
Someone
To save
Him

Do it for him

Like a
Helpless
Baby
Waiting
For another
To change
His
Diaper

For those

Driving in
Front
Of me
During the
Morning
Commute . . .

The gas pedal is on the right!

Patience

They say . . .
Is a virtue
But it is
Still not one
Of God's
10 Commandments

That means

I still have
A
Shot
To get
To heaven

Has

Something tragic
Ever happened
To someone
You know
And your
First thought
Is

I'm glad
It
Wasn't me?

You've got it

All wrong
You know

It was an act
Of honesty
From the beginning

It's true
That I'm not the biggest fan
Of the Almighty

But in that garden
As I slithered around
That Tree
I was trying to save them

Poor Adam and Eve
Innocent
But equally ignorant

They were given one rule
To refrain from
Eating the fruit
Without ever knowing
Why

They were created
Without any knowledge
Of good and evil

Which begs me
To encourage you
To consider
The fact
They were made
"In his likeness"

No understanding
Of
Happiness and Punishment

Existent
Pointless
Machines

Surviving
In a paradise they could
Never appreciate

And now everyone
Demonizes me
"Literally"
For simply
Telling her
The truth

I removed her blindfold
And now everyone hates me for it

Her creator kept her
In the dark
Didn't want her

Didn't want him
To know

They were no different than the
Vacant
Plants
The obtuse animals they
"Ruled"
Over

I saved them

Yes
I know that pain
Suffering
And their inevitable
Eradication
Was part of the process

But it gave meaning to their existence

What is joy
Without the potential for
Anguish?

What is accomplishment
Without the possibility of
Failure?

What is life
Without the necessity
Of death?

Without Eve
And Adam's
Inherent curiosity
From God

Like God . . .

Their life had no
Principle

Neither did
God's

And neither
Did yours

All I have left to say is . . .

You are most welcome

1944

The day after Christmas
In the small village
Of Sommocolonia
He was surrounded

Trapped
On the second floor
Trapped
In a sea
Of sharks

All allies had withdrawn

We often
Refer to men
In this position
As being fearless
But this was not the case
For Lt. John Fox

He was terrified

But
Death
Was not the producer of
His fear

This was the deafening
Biblical moment
An administration of the final test

If the
Nazis were able
To take the position
The repulsive ideology
Would prevail

Fox's fear rested in defeat
In Evil's ability to win over Good

"Fire it!
There's more
Of them
Than there are
Of us.
Give them hell!"

These were
His final words
As he called the
Barrage of artillery fire on his own
Position

When he was found
Lt. John Fox was dead
Surrounded
By the
Lifeless remains
Of 100 German soldiers

We've broken everything

You know?

He sat on the

Park bench
Rocking back and forth
As the black tar
Drifted through
His veins
With the grace
Of all of
The angels from heaven

Like the grinding
Of tiny shards of glass
Making
Therapeutic
Cuts
That soothe

His mother
Cries with every
Convulsion of the eyes
Flutter of
The face
That her son experiences
There
On the park bench

His father
Blames himself
With every
Spasm of the
Neurological misfires
Of radiance
That happens
Right there
On the
Park Bench

His daughter
... Fragmented
Waits for the phone call
Waits for death
Each moment
Of
Disintegration
As he vacations
There
On that
Park bench

With each treatment
With each moment of deliverance
He sleeps
He suffocates
There
On the Park bench

When War

Has rules
The winner
Will always be
The one
Who ignored
Them

I told you so . . .

Is exactly what
I'll be saying
When your desire
To satisfy
Your laziness
Overpowers
The desire to
Produce
And all
That is left
Is dependence

She stood there . . .

So
I pretended like she wasn't

When I found out
He had died
I knew that
I had to go
And pay
What would be
My final respects

And I knew
That she'd be there

I stood
In line
Looking at pictures
Waiting for my
Turn
To see
The Dead
On Display

But that wasn't the
Worst of it

I knew she was in the line
Waiting
With family
To speak to those
Wishing
All the best

It had been 20
Years
Since I had seen
Since I had spoken to her

So
I tried
To pretend she wasn't

The plan was
To move on
Move away
Cease to exist
As I had done for so long

I stepped into the line
I shook the man's hand
The son of
The deceased
And said, "I'm sorry for
Your loss."
As we've all said
A thousand times
. . . or more

He responded with
"Have you met my wife?"
And so I glanced
Into that mirror

Into her face
And it looked exactly
Like mine

I'm not sure

How he knew
But he could tell
That the room
Was lit up
Even though he couldn't see

Come to think of it
His whole head was covered
It was a black
Fiber
Whose material
Touched the inside
Of his mouth
Every time
He took
An obstructed breath
As if he were drowning

Torture
Is what he thought
"I am about to be
Tortured."

The idea
Rushed through the blood
Vessels in his neck
To the humid

Face
Under the saturated fabric

A rainforest of terror

His hands
Were bound tightly
Behind his back
Where he could feel
The fingers begin to numb
Mobility and sensation
Lost

But it couldn't be too bad
He was still standing
He was not completely tied down
He could walk
If he wanted

It was his decision
To remain stationary

Motionless
He could hear
One subtle sound
The sound
Of many others
Struggling to breath
Through the
Full-faced covering

He could tell
From the direction of the noises
That he
Was standing side
By side

In a line
More like fence posts
As opposed to dominoes

And then he heard another sound
He was relieved when he
Realized
That it wasn't a scream
No sign of torment
No sign of struggle

Then there
Was a slight gurgling sound
The sound of trickling fluid (probably just water)
Followed by a thud

Harmless sounds
Like someone had dropped
A heavy bag
On the floor

Or what was once
A living body
Capable of thinking
For itself

Driving

Everyday
From one
Lifeless world
To another
And then back
Again

It's funny

I remember
When
I was young
How amazed I
Was
When you took a rubber band
And without breaking it,
"Tied the two ends
Together"

"Watch this"
As you snuck
The band
Behind your back
Used a little magic
Twisted it twice
Then held it back out front
Locking the two ends
Together

It was an illusion
Just a trick

You said
Life keeps getting harder

You were right
. . . It does

And when life does
Get harder

Just like you

I use a little magic
Try not to break it
And tie the two ends
Together

But seriously . . .

What are you
Doing here?

www.ingramcontent.com/pod-product-compliance
Lightning Source LLC
LaVergne TN
LVHW051648080426
835511LV00016B/2552